Intelligent Writing with AI

How to Master Technology to Enhance Literary Creativity

Intelligent Writing with AI

How to Master Technology to Enhance Literary Creativity

José Manuel González

ISBN: 9798329630466
Independently published

Cover Design: JMGC Books
Cover Image: Dall-E
Layout: JMGC Books
Safe Creative Registration Number: 2406278407165

To all those who dare to dream

"The future is hidden behind the men who make it."

Anatole France

INTRODUCTION

Welcome to the dawn of a new chapter in the art of writing. Whether you're advancing page by page through the digital version of this book or resting with the physical edition on your lap, it's the curiosity about Artificial Intelligence (AI) that has brought you here.

You might be wondering how you and AI can forge the future of 21st-century literature together. You are about to dive into the answer, or at least, the right path to clear your doubts. Are you ready to radically transform your way of writing, thinking, and creating? Get ready, because this journey promises to be as surprising as if your morning coffee decided to prepare itself. Or your tea, because there is room for everything in this world.

At this very moment, while you turn the first pages of this book from your favorite reading nook, you might be asking yourself: "AI in writing? Isn't that for technophiles and visionaries?" Let me assure you of one thing: the future is already here, and it is loaded with unimaginable possibilities. AI isn't exclusively reserved for robot dreamers, alternate realities, or those who wonder if androids dream of electric sheep; it's for everyone who desires narratives that resonate with the soul, stories that challenge our imagination, and articles that... well, keep us awake instead of putting us to sleep on the keyboard.

The revolution of AI in creative writing doesn't seek to replace your genius with binary code. On the contrary, it's like having a personal assistant who never complains, doesn't need rest, and most importantly, doesn't judge your late-night drafts. Imagine it: while you dedicate yourself to building universes with your words, which is what you really want to do, your tireless AI companion will be there to suggest the perfect synonym that your tired brain can't remember, that phrase that doesn't quite sound right, or change that awful dialogue you just wrote that seems unrealistic.

And if you're worried about how this bond with AI will affect your precious creative process, let me ease your fears. The real magic happens when you combine your creativity with AI, bringing to life stories that no one, not even you, would have imagined possible. And although you might initially think this is the most improbable alliance, it won't take long to realize that they are actually the perfect complement. One for the other.

This book is designed to change the game for you. Not only will I explain how AI can enhance your writing, but also how you can preserve your unique and unrepeatable voice in the process. Get ready to explore new frontiers of creativity and efficiency, and who knows, you might discover a newfound hobby for technology and all the tools it puts at your disposal.

If you're ready to leap into the future of writing, you've come to the right place. Together, we are going to unveil the mysteries of AI and discover how it can become your most precious ally in the pursuit of literary excellence. And maybe, by the end of this journey, the idea of having your best friend as an artificial intelligence will bring a smile to your face.

Welcome to the exciting world of intelligent writing with AI. Let's begin.

Chapter 1

UNDERSTANDING ARTIFICIAL INTELLIGENCE

Fundamentals of AI

Before delving into the labyrinth of possibilities that AI offers us as storytellers, I invite you to pause, take a deep breath, and open your mind to this new horizon. It's not complicated, but it does require your full attention. Put your phone aside, just as you do when you set out to write your stories, and join me on this journey.

In the vast sea of Artificial Intelligence, where the waters alternate between calm and storm, it is essential to understand its fundamentals. I'm not one to build the roof before the foundations, are you?

But wait…

I wanted to compare it to the act of writing, where you usually don't start with the ending or do certain things before outlining your next novel. Although I know writers who sometimes have the ending before they start their story.

The purpose of this book is, at the very least, to make you lose your fear of AI. I promise that once you give it a chance, you will see your creativity and productivity multiply. If you're ready and willing, let's continue this adventure.

What exactly is Artificial Intelligence? To explain it simply and without technical details, AI is that writing companion you never knew you needed. Think of these powerful tools as entities capable of performing tasks that would normally require human intelligence and a lot of time. These tasks include understanding natural language (yes, even your late-night ramblings), recognizing patterns (like our tendency to look for synonyms for "said"), and learning from experience (without the temper tantrums).

But keep in mind: AI hasn't come to usurp the place of human editors, proofreaders, designers, or translators. In my opinion, it comes to reinforce all those tasks that used to take many hours and that now, with its help, you can perform more productively. And let's be realistic. The world spins at dizzying speeds, and if we want to stay in the market, we must be more efficient than our competitors.

What is clear is that AI will never be able to replace a human because it lacks a soul. And what is a work without a soul?

Nothing.

How does it work? Imagine you're teaching your dog to bring you the newspaper or your slippers. Over time, it will learn that, at your signal, it should pick up that pile of paper the boy on the bike throws into your yard every morning (well, maybe this happened in the eighties). AI operates similarly, but instead of newspapers, it works with data. A sea, an infinite ocean of data. Feed this beast enough examples, and it will learn to recognize patterns, make predictions, and, in the realm of writing, even suggest how to continue your intergalactic love saga or provide the necessary data for your latest essay.

Algorithms, those invisible friends. Think for a moment about a Harry Potter story: if AI were any of the wizards at Hogwarts, the algorithms would be their magic wands. They are the rules and procedures that guide Artificial Intelligence in its learning and decision-making. Everyone has heard about the algorithms that Amazon follows to recommend its products, the ones Instagram uses to make an account go viral, and all those stories; well, this is the same, only to guide AI. Some algorithms are simple, like following a recipe to the letter. Others are more complex, capable of adjusting their own rules as they learn from the data we provide with our conversations. It's as if the cake recipe adapted to become even more delicious each time you bake it, based on your own tastes. You know, practice makes perfect. AI, the same.

Machine Learning and Deep Learning, the prodigy brothers. This is where things get really interesting. But don't be scared, I'll only explain it briefly so you know these words and understand them. Machine Learning (ML) is a subset of AI that focuses on teaching machines to learn from data without being explicitly programmed for each task. If we continue with the dog example, imagine teaching your dog new tricks simply by rewarding it each time it does something right. Deep Learning, on the other hand, is a type of ML that uses neural networks with many layers. These networks try to mimic the way the human brain processes information, allowing them to learn incredibly complex tasks. In this way, it can learn incredibly complex tasks. What I tell you, we're not just talking about a dog fetching the newspaper but also being able to make you coffee. Can you imagine?

And what does all this mean for you, my dear writer? It means you will have at your disposal a powerful tool that can learn from your writing style, offer suggestions based on all the literary data it already has, and help you explore new creative directions. AI is here to serve you, inspire you, and maybe, just maybe, keep you company during those long writing nights.

So, as we prepare to take these tools by the hand and realize how AI is changing the writing landscape, remember: We are on the brink of a new era of creativity, and this is just the beginning. With the fundamentals of AI firmly under our command, we are ready to explore how this fascinating technology can become your muse, your editor, and your most trusted collaborator.

How AI is Changing the Writing Landscape

Now that we've built a solid foundation of knowledge about the fundamentals of AI and are confidently floating over the waters of technology, it's time to navigate how this wave of innovation can redefine our literary landscape. Yes, dear reader, AI is not only changing the game but creating a completely new one with new rules.

The assistant you always dreamed of. Imagine having an assistant who not only brings you coffee (it won't, though that would be impressive) but also offers plot suggestions, helps with research, develops characters, and checks your grammar and spelling without judging you for those mistakes you make when you can't go on anymore. AI is here to do all that for you, quickly, thoroughly because it is trained for it, and without complaining. Thanks to advanced tools, it is now possible to have a writing companion who understands your needs and adapts to the style that makes you unique and unmistakable.

Goodbye, writer's block. Remember those times when the words just wouldn't flow? Well, AI is also here to change that. With tools capable of suggesting ideas, developing plot lines, and even generating convincing dialogues, the dreaded writer's block could become a thing of the past. It's like having a writing fairy godmother, ready to sprinkle her creative magic when you need it most. And we've all had that feeling of not being able to get a single word out. Well, that's over. Chat with AI for a moment, and it will make everything flow again.

Personalization at its peak. One of the most exciting changes AI is bringing to the writing world is the ability to personalize content like never before. Whether adapting a book to resonate better with certain readers or creating versions of stories that fit different cultures or interests, AI is opening doors to a world of personalized possibilities.

Efficiency and speed. Too many ideas and too little time? Are you self-published and need help with everything? AI to the rescue. With its ability to assist in research, plot structuring, and draft revisions, AI can mean the difference between meeting those impossible deadlines or not. It's like having an extra speed boost in your pen, allowing you to produce more without compromising quality. In a world that moves faster and faster, having an assistant that makes your work more productive becomes increasingly necessary. And what about marketing processes, cover ideas, advertising, and those things that often escape us? AI will also be able to help you with those tasks.

A new horizon of creativity. A New Horizon of Creativity. But perhaps the most exciting thing of all is how AI is pushing the boundaries of our creativity. With access to a vast network of information and the ability to learn from countless sources, AI can inspire us to explore themes, genres, and styles we never considered before. It is not only expanding our literary world but also enriching our imagination. For example, I am mainly a thriller and suspense author, although I have several pseudonyms with which I write in other genres and types of books. In my showcase, there are fiction and non-fiction books, books to learn, and others for children. With the help of AI, I have turned my passion for writing into my way of life.

In summary, AI is transforming the writing landscape in ways we are just beginning to understand. From being a personal assistant to opening new paths to creativity, AI is quickly becoming an indispensable ally for writers of all genres and styles. And as we face this new era together, who knows what other literary wonders await us on the horizon. So, keep your mind open, your curiosity alive, and your keyboard ready, because the adventure of writing with AI has just begun.

Set Realistic Goals. AI can be powerful, but it still can't write your novel while you sleep (although who knows, the future is long and full of mysteries). Because yes, you've heard that there are already numerous books on the market completely created by an AI. But that's not what you and I want, right? Not at least, I don't. I'm a writer, so I'm passionate about writing. I turn to AI when looking for ideas for new plots, generating outlines, first ideas, sketches, and all that. It helps me when I need to make a voice sound a certain way, to learn about historical moments that would take time to study, visit places, and those kinds of things. However, be realistic about what you can achieve with these tools and what you really want to do. Set attainable goals and give it time. Integrating AI into your writing process is a marathon, not a sprint, just like finishing a novel of sixty or seventy thousand words.

Prepare to Learn. Yes, even old dogs can learn new tricks. Using AI in your writing may require you to acquire some new technical skills. But don't let that scare you. Think of it as learning to ride a bike: at first, you might wobble a bit, but soon you'll be pedaling confidently, enjoying the wind in your face and the freedom that comes with mastering a new skill. And trust me, once you get the hang of the tools you acquire, you'll move to a new level of creativity and productivity. Don't despair if you don't get what you're looking for at first. Just like you have to learn to know the different AI tools, it will also have to learn from you to give you what you need at each moment and situation.

In summary, preparing to integrate AI into your writing process is like planning an epic journey (or a novel). You need to know where you want to go, what tools you'll bring with you, and be willing to learn and adapt along the way. So, as you buckle up and prepare to take off toward this new creative horizon, remember: the journey of a thousand pages begins with a single click (of the mouse and your mind).

With this strategic, personalized, and hopefully a bit fun approach, you're ready to make AI your writing companion, exploring new peaks of creativity together. Forward, brave writer, the future of writing awaits you!

Selecting the Right AI Tools for Writers

Ah, the choice of tools! Here we are at the AI supermarket with an empty cart, ready to fill it with the best technological goodies. But wait, how do we decide what to take? Not all AI tools are created equal, and we definitely don't want to end up with a can of alphabet soup when what we were looking for was the secret ingredient for our next bestseller. And for that, it was crucial that you did a first evaluation of needs since it's not the same to need a writing assistant as to only want someone to take care of your advertising or marketing, create your covers, and things like that. However, if you're reading this book, you're mainly interested in a writing assistant. So, buckle up; we're going to navigate the aisles of this digital supermarket.

Know Your Literary Diet. First, think about what you need. If your writing were a diet, would it be high in adventure, rich in mysteries, or balanced with a little bit of everything? Identify the areas where you feel an AI tool could help you. Do you need an idea generator to spice up your stories? Or perhaps a grammatical assistant to ensure your sentences flow like the Amazon River? (Wink). An all-in-one? A tool that serves only to generate articles for my blog? Knowing what you need is the first step to filling your cart with the right tools without wasting too much time.

Read the Labels. Not literally, but do your research. Each AI tool comes with its own set of features, advantages, and yes, also limitations. Look for reviews, compare functions, and if possible, try demos or trial versions because some applications might be free and give you what you need, but others are paid and we also don't have to spend for the sake of spending. It's like tasting a piece of cheese in the store; you want to make sure it will perfectly complement your literary diet and pair well with that boisterous wine you bought days ago.

Compatibility with Your Creative Kitchen. Make sure the tool integrates well with your current writing process. If you're a night owl writer who primarily uses an old laptop, perhaps you don't need an AI tool that requires the latest hardware technology. The perfect tool is one that feels like an extension of your own creativity, not like a robot intruder in your sacred writing space. Think that if you don't choose well, your productivity will plummet. I'm telling you from experience. In the end, you'll end up spending more time getting to know each tool than the time gained from them.

Long-term Nutrition. Think about the future. An AI tool might seem like the perfect solution now, but will it still be useful as you grow and evolve as a writer? Look for tools that offer updates and ongoing support. Technology advances rapidly, and you want a travel companion that can keep pace. Likewise, don't be afraid to try out new tools if you see that the current ones no longer meet your needs. But be very careful because I repeat the same thing as before: It should not take up all your time.

Budget. Yes, money. Those AI tools aren't always cheap, but you also don't need to break the bank to get a good one. Many of them have free options that might be more than enough for what you're looking for or need. Set a budget and look for the best option within your limits. Remember, the best tool is the one you can afford to use without it leaving you living off instant noodles for the rest of the month. In fact, you have to think of tools as a small investment to grow your writing and, if you wish, also your editorial and creative business. Many times, we think that the most expensive tools with the options most desired by everyone are the best option. Nothing could be further from the truth. Maybe you only need a little push to make this craft your profession and generate more content or quality books. For that, the free version of that software might be enough.

Join the Community. Writing can be a solitary activity, but that doesn't mean you have to navigate the world of AI alone. Join online forums, social media groups, or online communities where other writers share their experiences with different AI tools. It's like a book club but instead of discussing the latest psychological thriller, you're exchanging notes on the latest AI technology. In those places, you can find out if a tool will serve you well for one purpose or for a very different one. And I can tell you, in those places, books are always talked about, which is ultimately what matters to all of us. There, you might make great friends and companions in letters with your same concerns.

Selecting the right AI tool is like choosing the perfect ingredient for your signature dish. It requires patience, research, and a bit of experimentation. But when you find that tool that syncs perfectly with your writing style, transforming your ideas into literary masterpieces, you'll know all the effort was worth it. So, go ahead, brave literary explorer, the AI supermarket is open and ready for you to discover its treasures.

Chapter 3

OVERCOMING INITIAL CHALLENGES

Handling Expectations

So, you've decided to embark on the exciting journey of AI-assisted writing. Congratulations! You're about to dive into a world where technology meets creativity, sparking ideas that could light up an entire night sky. (Pretty, right?). But before you plunge headfirst, expecting to swim in a sea of perfect prose and effortless plots, let's talk about something important: managing your expectations.

AI is not a magic wand. I know, I know, we all want to believe in magic, especially when it comes to overcoming writer's block, finding the exact word that's been dancing on the tip of our tongue, or finishing a novel (or two) in record time. But the truth is, as advanced as AI may be, it's not going to write your novel overnight while you're out having drinks with friends. Consider AI as a workout buddy at the gym; it can motivate you, guide you, and help you lift those heavy blocks of writing, but you're the one who has to do the hard work. In fact, don't leave everything to AI because, as I said before, it lacks a soul. Your soul.

Set realistic goals. I've already talked about this before. I warned you that you should set realistic goals with AI tools and their learning. With writing, it's the same. Imagine you're learning to play a musical instrument. You wouldn't expect to play like Beethoven in your first week, right? (And if you do, well, I applaud your optimism). It's the same with AI. Start with small goals, like improving your writing speed or generating ideas for articles on your literary blog, generating more precise plots in less time, or streamlining the necessary documentation process. As you become more familiar with the tools and what they can do, you can adjust your expectations and goals.

The learning curve. Here comes the fun part: learning to use new tools. And by "fun," I mean the kind of fun you feel when trying to assemble furniture while looking at instructions that seem to have been written in an alien language or by a Buddhist monk on a kilometric stone wall. But fear not, perseverance is key. Dedicate time to understand how your chosen AI tool works. Experiment with it, play, make mistakes. Remember, even great inventors had to deal with countless failures before achieving success.

Personalization takes time. And here we reach the true goal. You want your AI tool to understand your unique voice, your style, your quirks; to help you create the promotional campaign you need at each moment, the article that defines you in your niche, all while maintaining your unique and unmistakable voice. This won't happen overnight. Feed your AI with examples of your writing, adjust its settings, talk to it (yes, talking to your AI is perfectly fine, we won't judge). Indeed, that's exactly what you have to do. Over time, you'll find that your digital assistant begins to reflect your personal style more closely, like a technological mirror of your creativity.

Celebrate every victory. Every time your AI tool helps you overcome an obstacle, celebrate it, just as you do when you finally put the finishing touches on that work that has trapped you for months. Whether it's finding the perfect word that eluded your memory or suggesting a secondary plot that breathes new life into your story, these small victories are not only rewarding but also motivate you to continue exploring and making the most of this unique collaboration.

In summary, the journey toward AI-assisted writing is full of possibilities, learning, and yes, also some stumbles. But by managing your expectations realistically and approaching this journey with an open mind and adventurous spirit, you'll find yourself discovering new depths of creativity you may never have known existed. So adjust your sails, persevering writer, the wind of AI blows strong and will carry you to new creative horizons.

Overcoming Technical Ignorance and Option Overload

Here you are, standing at the edge of the vast jungle of AI technology, armed only with your wit and, perhaps, a cup of coffee (or two, who's counting?). Technical ignorance and the overwhelming array of options can seem like formidable beasts in this jungle, but fear not, for you are about to become an expert in navigating this technological maze with the grace of a cat and the cunning of Sherlock Holmes.

Taming Technical Ignorance. Remember the first time you tried to ride a bike? It was probably a bit scary. But with practice and patience, you got the hang of it. The same principle applies here. Start with the basics. There's an ocean of resources available: online tutorials, video tutorials, free online courses on AI, webinars, and more. Dedicate a little time each day to learn something new about each specific AI. Think of it as your morning workout, but for your brain. However, don't spend all your time on it, as if you do, you won't write, which is the most important thing of all. Ah! And when you've been beating your brains for a while, drop everything and go do some sport. You'll thank me.

Navigating Option Overload. Imagine you're at a gigantic buffet. You can't possibly try everything (though some might try), so how do you choose? This is where understanding your own needs and goals comes into play (see Chapter 2). Filter options through the sieve of your needs. Do you need help with grammar and spelling? Look for tools specifically designed for that. Want to generate story ideas? There's likely an app for that. Use your objectives as a compass to guide you through this buffet of technology. Now, yes, you should be a writer with a map, not letting yourself be led by an unknown compass that makes you lose your way among so many options.

The Small Plate Technique. Instead of overwhelming yourself trying to learn about all the available tools at once, start small. Pick one or two tools that seem most relevant to your current needs and dive deep into them. Think that, as you did before, make a plan of needs and look for those tools that help you in those tasks, not more. Master those tools before adding others to your arsenal. It's like building your own tasting menu of AI technology, one dish at a time.

Join a Community. You're not alone in this jungle. Many other writers are navigating the same uncharted territory. Look for online forums, Facebook groups, or Reddit communities where people share tips, tricks, and recommendations about AI tools. These communities can be beacons of light in the fog of option overload, offering you guidance and support. And if that overwhelms you, talk to me. Don't hold back. Write me an email, and I'll help you in this new stage of your writing career. I'll show you how I do it and what tools I've chosen in my journey.

Celebrating Small Achievements. Every time you learn something new, take a moment to celebrate. Managed to write your first draft with the help of an AI tool? Congratulations! Found a hidden feature in your writing software that saves you time? That deserves a victory dance or a good beer. These small celebrations not only motivate you to keep going but also reinforce your learning.

Remember, overcoming technical ignorance and the overload of options is not a race; it's a journey. A journey full of discovery, growth, and yes, also a bit of frustration. But with each step you take, you're better equipped to make the most of AI's potential in your writing. So go ahead, adjust your explorer's hat, and step into the jungle with confidence. Great literary adventures await you. And also to the future readers of your stories.

Chapter 4

ENHANCING CREATIVITY
WITH AI

Inspiration and Idea Generation

Welcome to the digital muse's workshop, where ideas flow as freely as coffee on a writer's morning. If you've ever found yourself staring at a blank page, wondering where all the good ideas have gone—be it from the night before, the previous day, last week, the last book, or a previous life—I have good news for you. AI is here to be your lantern in the dark, your GPS through the desert of creativity, or that red thread connecting you to the muses. Let's explore how these wonderful tools can help you find an oasis of inspiration where you least expect it.

Igniting the Creative Spark: Think of AI as that friend who always has the best ideas but without the need to be treated to coffee. Tools powered by AI can generate titles, story concepts, and even complete plots based on a few parameters you provide. Need a love story set on Mars? A psychological thriller with an unexpected twist? AI can give you that starting point. And the best part is, it won't get offended if you decide to take a completely different direction because, suddenly, those elusive muses show up.

The "What If...?" Game: One of the most enjoyable ways to use AI for generating ideas is the "What If...?" game. Input a series of scenarios into your AI tool, each more absurd or intriguing than the last, and see how it responds. These are the kinds of irrelevant, absurd questions you wouldn't ask a professional editor out of embarrassment but would ask a machine. What if cats ruled the world? What if you could read your boss's mind? The responses can not only serve as the beginning of a great story but also as an excellent way to stretch your creative muscles.

Breaking Through Blocks: Sometimes, writer's block arises simply because we're too close to our work. Or out of fear—that's another reason. This is where AI can be a game changer. By offering unexpected suggestions or unique angles, it can help you see your project from a new perspective. It's like having a collaborator who comes without any preconceived notions or assumptions about your work. With it, your ego will never be hurt.

Exploring Genres: Have you ever wanted to experiment with a genre outside your comfort zone but didn't know where to start? AI can guide you on that journey. By generating ideas or plots within specific genres, it gives you a foundation to build upon. It's a safe way to dip your toes into the waters of new genres without the fear of drowning.

Co-Creation: Lastly, but certainly not least, consider AI as a co-creator. By working together, you can come up with ideas that you would never have considered on your own. It's not a competition; it's more of a collaboration. AI provides a canvas full of possibilities, but you're the one who adds color and life to the picture. Don't forget that.

AI is revolutionizing how we find inspiration and generate ideas. By embracing these tools, you're not just opening the door to a world of creative possibilities; you're also inviting a burst of innovation into your writing. So, the next time you feel stuck, remember: inspiration might just be a click away, waiting on the digital wings of that new AI tool.

Improving Workflow and Overcoming Writer's Block

Ah, writer's block: that age-old adversary of pens, pencils, keyboards, and the human spirit alike. It visits all of us at some point, like that unwelcome distant relative showing up at family gatherings or the metaphorical "man with the hammer" for cyclists on an endless mountain pass. But fear not, for I come bearing a master plan to transform this unwanted visitor into a source of inspiration, all thanks to our beloved AI. Let's dive into how this marvelous technology can not only enhance your workflow but also send you soaring over the wall of writer's block.

First, Organize Your Creative Chaos: AI can be your digital Marie Kondo, helping you sort through your ideas, notes, and drafts. AI-based organization tools can categorize your work, suggest improvements, and most importantly, help you keep track of those flashes of genius that would otherwise get lost in the abyss of unsaved documents. It's like having a personal assistant who understands your creative mind better than you do.

Set a Rhythm: We all have those days when writing feels like trying to run through a swamp. This is where AI can step in and act as your personal coach. Apps that monitor your progress, offer personalized goals, and give you that motivational boost when you need it most can be game-changers. No more excuses for procrastination; it's time to set a pace that even Hemingway would envy.

Goodbye Writer's Block: Now to the heart of the matter. When faced with the daunting wall of writer's block, AI has a toolbox full of gadgets to help you knock it down. From serving as a potent idea generator to acting as a writing assistant that suggests how to proceed with your story, AI can provide that spark needed to reignite your creativity. Think of it as a defibrillator for your dying muse. Ask it about that plot that's become too tangled, that character who seems to have lost their voice in the story, or that narrative voice. You'll see, AI will eliminate the block with new and inspiring ideas.

Inspiration on Demand: Ever wished you could press a button and receive an instant dose of inspiration? Well, with AI, you almost can. AI tools can immerse you in a sea of art, literature, and science to inspire you. Whether you need a setting for your next scene or to understand the psychology behind a character, AI can bring that information to you on a silver platter, feeding your creative process with a constant flow of fresh ideas.

Refining Your Voice: AI doesn't just help you overcome writer's block; it can also refine your voice, ensuring that every word, sentence, paragraph, and book resonates with clarity and power. AI-based editing tools can suggest stylistic improvements, helping you polish your work until it shines. It's like having an editor in your back pocket, always ready to help you fine-tune your craft. Remember, it's common for writers to sound different at the beginning of a story than at the end. Writers change from one day to the next, imagine from one month to the next. AI is going to change that in a flash (pun intended). On one hand, it will make you write your drafts faster by having fewer blocks, so the passage of time won't be as noticeable in your pen. On the other hand, you can ask it to equalize the style of both parts. It will do it without grumbling.

In summary, AI is here to transform your writing workflow from a series of obstacles into a smooth, well-oiled racetrack. With the help of this technology, you can say goodbye to writer's block, organize your creative chaos, and find the inspiration that propels you forward. So, the next time that old enemy tries to pay you a visit, you'll be more than prepared to welcome it with a smile and an arsenal of AI tools that will turn that challenge into your next great work.

Chapter 5

MAINTAINING ORIGINALITY AND QUALITY

Ensuring Content Authenticity

In a world where AI is on the verge of writing novels that would make Dostoevsky green with envy (or so we like to imagine), a critical question arises: How do we maintain our unique voice and ensure that our work remains genuinely ours? Well, get ready, because we're going to dive into the art of balancing technology and authenticity, ensuring that your work shines with its own light even in the digital age.

The Voice that Distinguishes You. First and foremost, let's remember that AI is a tool, not a substitute. I suppose you have this clear, especially if you actually enjoy writing. Think of it as a brush in Van Gogh's hands; it's the artist, not the brush, that creates the magic. Similarly, AI can help you explore new horizons and polish your work, but your voice—that unique spark that distinguishes you—comes from you and no one else. And it must stay that way. So, while using these tools, keep injecting your experiences, emotions, and perspective into every word. Remember: AI lacks a soul. Don't look for advice in this book to leave everything in the hands of these tools because you won't find it. I AM A WRITER. And so are you.

Maximum Personalization. Most AI tools allow a certain degree of customization. Take advantage of it. Feed the AI with examples of your previous work, play with the settings until you feel the suggestions it offers resonate with your desired personal style. It's a bit like training a puppy to become the perfect companion; it requires patience and consistency, but the result is worth it, I assure you.

Innovate, Don't Imitate. Yes, AI can give you access to a vast library of styles and genres. But here's the trick: use it to inspire, not to imitate. You don't want to sound like everyone else because you'll sell one day and bore for the rest. Keep being original and creative. If a tool suggests a phrase that sounds more like Shakespeare than you, take it as a springboard to find your own expression. Originality comes from reinterpretation and reinvention, not repetition.

Quality as Your Compass. In the eagerness to produce more and faster, don't lose sight of the quality of your work for even a second. AI can help you generate content at impressive speeds, but it's you who must ensure that each piece maintains the standard you've set. Take the time to review, edit, and, if necessary, rewrite. Think of AI as a kitchen assistant who prepares the ingredients, but you are the chef who ensures the final dish is a masterpiece worthy of several Michelin stars. And don't be afraid to remake it if it doesn't taste right.

Human Feedback, the Final Key. Last but definitely not least, never underestimate the value of human feedback. No matter how advanced your AI tool is, the opinion of real readers, editors, and fellow writers is invaluable and irreplaceable. They can catch nuances, emotions, and connections that AI, for now, cannot. And realistically, let's hope it never can.

Ensuring authenticity and quality in the AI era is ultimately a balancing act. It's about making the most of the tools available without losing sight of what makes you unique as a writer. Therefore, as you advance in this exciting journey alongside technology, remember that the heart of your work should always be yours. No tricks, no cheats, because I assure you that your readers will notice immediately.

Editing and Polishing AI-Generated Texts

Now that we've mastered the art of maintaining our authentic voice in the age of AI, it's time to put on the editor's hat and polish those texts until they shine like a literary crown jewel. Yes, I know this part might not excite you too much, but even diamonds need to be cut and polished, and AI-generated texts are no exception. Let's dive into the world of literary refinement, where every word counts and every sentence has the potential to be a masterpiece.

The First Rule of the Editing Club: You're the Boss. When it comes to editing AI-generated texts, remember that you have the final say. The AI can suggest, but the power of decision rests with you. It's like being the conductor of an orchestra; the AI can provide the music, but you decide the rhythm, tone, and volume. Don't be afraid to deviate from the script, change a word here, adjust a sentence there. At the end of the day, the text should resonate with your voice, not the machine's. In fact, this can only be seen from one perspective: the machine helps, but you are the one who does the real work.

Diving Deep. Editing goes beyond correcting grammatical or punctuation errors. It's about diving deep into your text, examining each idea, each argument, ensuring that everything flows in a more or less coherent way. Ask yourself: Does this sound like something I would write? Does this section add value to my narrative? Don't settle for the surface; dive into the depths. In the end, you'll have a first draft of your text ready to present to a professional proofreader or editor. It is that person, and only they, who will truly polish your text.

The Art of Cutting. Whether you're a fiction or non-fiction writer, you must cut to the bone. Sometimes, less is more. What am I saying, sometimes: ALWAYS. This is especially true in editing AI-assisted texts. Technology can be prone to verbosity, producing more words than necessary. Don't be afraid to wield a sharp knife and cut what doesn't serve. Each word in your text should have a purpose, contribute to the narrative, or enrich the description. If it doesn't, it's time to say goodbye. Don't lose sight of the real purpose of AI, which is to serve as an assistant.

Consistency is Your Friend. Maintaining a consistent voice throughout an AI-assisted text can be a challenge, but it's crucial for the quality of your work. Ensure that the style and tone are consistent from start to finish. If your AI tool tends to suggest stylistic variations, take the time to smooth out those rough patches. You want your reading to be a smooth journey, not a ride down a bumpy road.

Feedback, Feedback, and More Feedback. Once you've run your text through the editing mill, seek external opinions. Sometimes we're so close to our work that we're blind to obvious mistakes or necessary improvements. Feedback from trusted friends, fellow writers, or even a beta reader group can be invaluable. Listen to their comments, absorb what makes sense, and use that information to put the finishing touches on your work.

Editing and polishing AI-generated texts is a meticulous but necessary and incredibly rewarding process. In the end, you'll not only have improved the quality of your work but also deepened your understanding and skill as a writer. So, with editing tools in hand and a critical eye, go forth and transform those drafts into the literary gems they were destined to be.

Chapter 6

PERSONALIZATION AND STYLE

Adapting AI to Your Unique Voice

You've arrived at the exciting world of personalization, where AI meets the essence of your creative being to dance to the rhythm of your unique voice. Imagine for a moment that AI is a chameleon, capable of changing its colors to match your individual style. Yes, this means you don't have to settle for generic texts that sound like they were written by a robot on its first day of work. Let's discover how you can teach this wonderful digital creature to sing in your voice.

Total Immersion. The first step to adapting AI to your style is to immerse it in the world of your writing. Feed your AI tool examples of your previous work, especially those you are particularly proud of. It's like training a new furry friend in the art of bringing you your favorite slippers; it needs to know which slippers those are before it can get it right.

Fine-Tuning and Feedback. Most AI tools come with a series of dials and controls you can adjust. Play with them. Do you prefer short, punchy sentences like Hemingway? Or are you more of a fan of flowery descriptions like Faulkner? Adjust your AI tool's settings to reflect your preferences. And don't forget to give it feedback again. If something doesn't sound right, tell it, it won't get upset. AI can learn from its mistakes just like we do.

The Personal Touch. Once again, while AI can mimic your style, there will always be elements that distinguish you. Your humor, your insights, the way you see the world. Make sure to infuse your texts with these elements. AI can give you the canvas and the palette, but you are the artist, don't forget that. Don't just accept the first thing AI offers you; use it as a starting point to add your personal touch and your personal voice.

Consistency is Key. Maintaining a consistent voice when working with AI can be a real challenge, especially if you are using multiple tools. To avoid this, create a "style guide" for yourself that you can consult and refer to when working hand-in-hand with AI. Include examples of your best work, preferred phrases and constructions, and even words or phrases you tend to avoid. This will not only help maintain your style consistently but also serve as a reminder of your unique voice.

Practice Makes Perfect. As with any tool, the key to adapting AI to your unique voice lies in practice. The more you work with it, the better it will become at understanding and replicating your style. Don't be afraid to experiment, to try new settings and adjustments. Over time, you will develop a synergy with your preferred AI tool that will allow you to produce texts that are not only true to your voice but also enrich your creative process.

In conclusion, adapting AI to your unique voice is not only possible but also an exciting adventure full of creative potential. Through immersion, fine-tuning, personal touch, consistency, and practice, you can teach your digital assistant to sing in your tone, dance to your rhythm, and most importantly, write as closely as possible to you. So go ahead, be bold, be creative, and above all, be yourself. AI is ready to follow you to infinity and beyond.

Techniques for Maintaining Style Consistency

Ah, style consistency, that Holy Grail of writing that we all seek. Like a chef trying to maintain the flavor of their signature dish through each service, maintaining consistency in your style throughout a text can be both an art and a science. And when you throw AI into the mix, well, let's say it's like trying to teach that chef to cook with a new set of futuristic ingredients. But fear not, for I have some techniques up my sleeve that will help you maintain a bright and uniform style no matter how much you rely on your AI assistant.

Create a Personal 'Style Bible'. Before even opening your AI tool, take a moment to define your style. This can include everything from sentence structure to the type of humor you prefer, to how you approach dialogues and descriptions. Think of this as your personal style bible, a living document that you can consult and update as your style evolves. This will be your compass when working with AI, ensuring that each suggestion or edit contributes to your overall creative vision and maintains your unique style.

Use AI for Analysis, Not Just Creation. AI tools are not only useful for generating text; many can analyze your writing for style and consistency patterns. Use these capabilities to gain an objective view of your work. It's like having an editor who never sleeps, always ready to point out where you might be straying from your characteristic style. Similarly, it could suggest that you yourself have deviated from one chapter to another.

Revision is Your Friend. There is no substitute for human revision, especially when it comes to maintaining style consistency. After working with your AI tool, take the time to review the text with a critical eye and the knife of a ruthless assassin. And when you've finished swinging the guillotine, ask trusted friends or fellow writers who understand your voice and style to give their opinion. Sometimes a minor change suggested by someone else can make a big difference in how your text is perceived. The text is yours today but theirs for the rest of the days. Ultimately, it will be your readers who dictate whether your work resonates with them, and if you remain true to your voice or not.

Maintain Consistency in Characters and Settings. Besides consistency in prose, ensure that your characters and settings remain true to themselves throughout the narrative. Okay, I know characters evolve throughout the story, but let it be in a consistent way. AI tools can help you track characteristics, motivations, and backgrounds of your characters, as well as details of settings, to ensure everything stays consistent from beginning to end. Additionally, you can ask it to create a profile for each of them according to your guidelines before starting the story.

Constant Fine-Tuning. Working with AI is a dynamic process. As I said before, don't be afraid to adjust your tool's settings as you progress, based on the results you're getting. If you notice that certain AI suggestions deviate from what you're looking for, dive into the settings and make the necessary changes. It's a delicate dance between technology and human intuition, but with practice, you'll find the perfect balance.

Never Lose Sight of Your Voice. Last but not least, always remember that your unique voice is what makes your writing special. AI tools are incredibly powerful, but they are just that: tools. It is you who brings the heart, soul, and style to your work. Keep that at the center of everything you do, and your style consistency will shine through any technology you use.

Maintaining style consistency while using AI is definitely a challenge, but it's also an incredible opportunity to grow as a writer and hone your craft. With these techniques in your toolbox, you're ready to ensure that your style not only remains consistent but also evolves and enriches with the help of artificial intelligence.

Chapter 7

ETHICS AND AUTHORSHIP IN THE AI ERA

Ethical Considerations of AI-Assisted Writing

Ethics in the era of artificial intelligence is somewhat thorny ground. Here in this chapter, we will navigate the sometimes turbulent waters of the ethical considerations surrounding the use of AI in writing. Imagine you are on an expedition in search of the legendary treasure of "Lost Ethics," a place where technology and morality dance on a line as fine as a tightrope wire. Let's unravel this mystery together with humor and humanity, of course, though with all the respect such a topic deserves. It couldn't be done any other way.

The Big Question: Who is the Author? Ah, the eternal question of authorship. When a machine helps you write, who gets the credit? Is it teamwork, like Lennon and McCartney writing hits, or is it something more complex? The key here is transparency. Just like a magician who reveals (or doesn't) his tricks, being clear about how you use AI in your creative process is not only ethically sound but also fosters trust with your readers. Think of it like the ingredient label on your favorite snack; people like to know what they are consuming. Anyway, I must warn you that you will be criticized by many. Some will accuse you of having your texts generated by AI and not being your own, especially if your productivity and success grow, making you a successful author. Envy often brings this. It is what it is.

Navigating the Waters of Originality. With AI generating content at supersonic speeds, the question arises: How can we ensure that what we create is truly original? Here is where your moral compass comes into play. Use AI as a brush, not as a painter. Let it inspire, challenge, and assist you, but make sure that the heart of your work is undeniably yours. Yours. Yours. It's like cooking a family recipe; you might use modern utensils, but the unique flavor comes from you. (From my mom, actually).

The Copy-Paste Dilemma. In a world where "Ctrl+C, Ctrl+V" could be considered a skilled superpower, it's vital to remember that great power comes with great responsibility. The temptation to take what AI produces and use it unfiltered is real, but resisting it is key to maintaining integrity and sleeping well at night. Think of it like following a diet; just because you can eat chocolate cake for every meal doesn't mean you should. Balance your creative diet with healthy portions of originality and authenticity. Never forget that the real writer is you and only you. AI is just your creative assistant.

Respecting Copyrights. This is a minefield at the best of times, but it essentially boils down to respecting the work of others. AI can access a vast sea of content to generate ideas, but make sure that your use does not infringe on the rights of other creators. It's a bit like inviting friends to a party at your house; you want them to feel respected and valued, not used.

The Ethics of Sharing the Stage. In the end, acknowledge the role that AI plays in your creative process. It's okay. There are already books co-written by humans and machines gaining recognition on bestseller lists. It is what it is. Celebrating this collaboration, rather than hiding it, is not only ethically sound but also opens a new chapter in the history of literature. It's like forming a band with a robot; it might not understand the concept of an "encore," but it can definitely add something special to the show.

Navigating the ethical considerations of AI-assisted writing is an ongoing journey of reflection, honesty, and transparency. By keeping these principles at the heart of your work, you'll not only be respecting your readers and the broader community, but you'll also be paving the way for a future where technology and human creativity coexist in complete harmony. So go ahead, sail towards that ethical horizon, with your moral compass firmly in hand. Be honest. Always. In everything. For everything.

Copyright and Attribution

The enigma of copyright and attribution in the digital age is a puzzle that would make even the most veteran intellectual property lawyers sweat. But fear not, dear companion of letters, because we will unravel this mystery together, with the help of our trusty ethical flashlight and a bit of humor to light the way, you know.

The Dance of Copyright. Imagine for a moment that you are at a dance, but instead of dancers, you have AI-generated works of art and brilliantly composed texts. The question is, who leads the dance? The creator of the AI, the user who clicked "generate," or the AI itself? Here is where things get interesting. In most cases, copyright law favors the human behind the creation. However, it is crucial to give credit where it is due, especially if you are using an AI tool to bring your literary visions to life. Think of it like tipping the DJ for playing your favorite songs; it's a matter of respect and recognition.

Navigating the International Waters of Attribution. Now, let's talk about attribution. In an ideal world, every fragment of text generated by AI would come with a clear label of "made by a machine, polished by a human." But reality is more complicated. When using AI tools, be transparent about their role in your creative process. You don't need to include a disclaimer on every page, but acknowledging it in your preface or a note at the end can be an elegant gesture of transparency. It's like admitting that your "homemade" apple pie was made with a store-bought crust; it doesn't detract from the taste but keeps things clear and straightforward. Not lying about this is crucial. In fact, if you end up publishing on Amazon, the platform already requires us to be honest and state if any part of our text, cover, or translation was generated in whole or in part by artificial intelligence. I repeat: Be honest. It's fine, and if the company changes its policies tomorrow and reviews which texts were generated by AI and which were not, you will have been honest.

The Delicate Art of Citation. As in traditional writing, if your AI work is inspired by or directly incorporates copyrighted work, citing your sources is not only an act of good faith but also a legal necessity. In this new territory, where inspiration can be an amalgamation of thousands of sources processed by a machine, finding the right balance between inspiration and infringement is more crucial than ever. It's like juggling flaming books: you want to keep them in the air without getting burned.

And AI? Does it Have Rights? For now, the answer is no. AI, as impressive as it is, is still considered a tool, not an author with rights. However, we are navigating uncharted waters, and the conversations about the ethics and legality surrounding AI authorship are far from over. Stay informed, stay curious, and above all, stay ethical in your practices. I assure you it is the best way to ensure that your literary adventures remain both exciting and ethically sound.

Forging the Path Ahead. Ultimately, copyright and attribution in the era of AI are constantly evolving terrains. By addressing these issues with integrity, respect for the law, and a commitment to transparency, you are not only protecting your own work and reputation but also contributing to a more ethical and sustainable creative ecosystem.

So, as we move forward together in this new era of AI-assisted creativity, let us remember the importance of ethics, attribution, and yes, a bit of common sense. And humor, of course. After all, we are writing the rules of a new world, and what better way to do it than with a spirit of adventure, respect, and a smile on our faces.

Chapter 8

SUCCESS STORIES AND CASE STUDIES

Stories of Writers Who Have Successfully Integrated AI into Their Creative Process

Now let me take you to the gallery of visionaries, a tour through the lives of those bold writers who have taken the reins of AI to gallop across the vast fields of literary creativity. These are the stories of pioneers, artists, and dreamers who have found in AI not just a tool, but a partner to bolster their writing and productivity. Remember that this world moves at dizzying speeds; if you want to compete on equal terms, you must get on the AI train to be more productive.

The Novelist Who Defied Traditional Narrative. Imagine Alex, a novelist who, after several best-sellers, felt that his muse had gone on a long vacation without leaving an address. Or left with someone else, because muses do that too. But Alex stumbled upon an AI designed to generate complex plots and multidimensional characters. At first, he was skeptical—how could a machine understand the complexity of the human soul? But by collaborating with AI, Alex discovered new ways to weave stories, exploring angles and emotional depths that had previously eluded him. His next novel, a psychological thriller with AI-generated twists, received critical acclaim and redefined his career.

The Poet Who Found Her Rhythm. Then there's Daniela, a poet who struggled with impostor syndrome, believing she would never match the greats of literature. For her, rhymes had lost their tempo. By interacting with an AI that analyzed patterns in classical and modern poetry, she began to experiment with innovative structures and metrics. The AI became her digital muse, pushing her to explore unknown lyrical territories. Daniela published a collection that was praised for its freshness and boldness, demonstrating that tradition and innovation can dance together under the moon of creativity.

The Sci-Fi Chronicler. Meet Samuel, or Sam, as he prefers to be called. His passion for science fiction led him to write stories that explore dystopian futures and technological utopias. However, keeping up with the latest scientific advances was overwhelming. He wasted too much time researching. By using an AI that filtered and summarized cutting-edge articles in fields like artificial intelligence, biotechnology, and space exploration, Samuel could infuse his narratives with authentic and provocative details, earning the respect of fans and critics for his accuracy and creativity.

The Blogger Who Overcame Writer's Block. Let's not forget Jaime, a blogger who regularly faced the dreaded writer's block. The solution came in the form of an AI designed to propose content ideas based on emerging trends and sentiment analysis, all while keeping SEO in mind. What began as an experiment turned into an inexhaustible source of inspiration, allowing Jaime to produce relevant and engaging articles that resonated with his audience, increasing his following and establishing his blog as an authority in his niche. Today, he makes a living from it.

These success stories are both unreal and probable. They show us that, when used with consideration and creativity, AI can be a powerful ally in our writing process. These writers not only overcame their challenges but also opened new paths, demonstrating that the union between human and artificial intelligence can result in works of unexpected beauty and depth. And now, let me tell you about a real writer who uses AI for all of the above:

ME. Exactly, that's right. As you might imagine, I wouldn't venture to speak about artificial intelligence without having a deep understanding of it. I am a writer, and of that, you can be completely sure. I love sitting down to write stories and then sharing them with you. I dedicate myself to writing both fiction and non-fiction books under various pseudonyms. Similarly, I venture into novels of different genres: mystery, horror, romance… Of course, I use a different pseudonym for each and have managed to create a personal brand in many of them. In parallel, I run a literary podcast, manage the social media of my various alter egos, am a federated athlete, and many other things. What I am trying to say is that it would be impossible to cover all this without the help of artificial intelligence. AI applications are fundamental in my creative process; they assist me in character creation, plot development, and adding authenticity to my stories. They are an invaluable resource during the research phase, especially if the plot includes historical elements that require precision and knowledge. AI acts as my Community Manager, personal assistant, editorial collaborator, and even performs an initial basic review of my texts. Additionally, it provides ideas for blog articles, suggests content for the podcast, and a ton of other things that I will discover little by little. As I said before, this is just beginning.

With this, I want to highlight the crucial importance that artificial intelligence has in my creative process. As I mentioned earlier, we need to move quickly if we want to dedicate ourselves to this full-time and, in the process, earn the money that allows us to live. Because, let's be honest, authors also face that strange need to eat and pay bills.

So whether you're looking to revitalize your narrative, explore new genres, or simply find that lost spark, remember these stories. Let them inspire you to view AI not as a rival, but as a companion on your creative journey. And who knows, perhaps your story will be the next one told in the yearbook of AI-assisted literature.

Chapter 9

CONCLUSION

Final Thoughts and a Look Towards the Future of AI-Assisted Writing

Here we are, at the end of this fascinating journey through the wonders and challenges of AI-assisted writing. Like any good book, it's time to conclude not only to tie up loose ends but also to prepare us for the next adventure. So, get comfortable, perhaps with a cup of your favorite beverage in hand, whether it's coffee or tea (after all, tastes vary, and so do colors in a rainbow), and let's reflect together on the path we've traveled and the horizon that lies ahead.

The Journey Thus Far. We have explored everything from the basics of AI to how this technology can be an ally in our creative pursuit. We've seen inspiring success stories, essential ethical considerations, and of course, shared more than one laugh along the way. Or at least, I've tried. If there's one thing we've learned, it's that AI is not here to replace us but to enrich our toolkit, offering new ways to explore and express our ideas.

The Future is Written in Code... and in Heart. Looking ahead, the future of AI writing seems as boundless as our imagination. But one thing is certain: the essence of storytelling, the heart of our stories, will remain profoundly human. Technology will advance, tools will become more sophisticated, but it will be our emotions, experiences, and visions of the world that continue to bring the most captivating stories to life.

An Unprecedented Collaboration. magine a future where writers and machines collaborate as naturally as musicians in an orchestra, each bringing their unique strengths to create literary symphonies that transcend what we could achieve alone. From novels that delve into the depths of the human soul to poetry that intertwines the cosmic and the everyday, the possibilities are as numerous as the stars in the sky.

Challenges Ahead. Of course, the path will not be without obstacles. Issues of ethics, copyright, and originality will remain topics of debate and discussion. But these challenges also offer us the opportunity to reflect on what it means to be a creator in the 21st century, forging a new pact between art and technology, where both can flourish.

You are the Narrator of this New Era. At the end of the day, it is you, dear writer, who has the power to shape this future. With every word you write, with every story you tell, you build bridges between humanity and the machine, between heart and code. So, I invite you to embrace this new era with curiosity, courage, and above all, with the passion for storytelling that transcends through the centuries.

So here we say goodbye, but only for now. The story of AI writing is just beginning, and you are on the front lines with a pen, quill, Staedtler pencil number two, or keyboard in one hand and the future in the other. Who knows what wonders we will write together on the yet unwritten pages of this exciting chapter of human history?

Chapter 10

APPENDICES

Now comes an important part: the Appendices. This is not the typical end of the book where you only find acknowledgments and a faded photo of the author. No, sir. Here is where I equip you with everything you need to become a master writer in the AI era. Think of this as your magic backpack, filled with tools, star maps, and maybe the occasional chocolate bar (because what adventure isn't improved with chocolate?). Let's dive in.

Recommended Resources: AI Tools, Tutorials, and Online Communities

AI Tools for Writers: Imagine you have a utility belt like Batman's, but instead of batarangs and grappling hooks, it's equipped with the most sophisticated AI tools.

OpenAI CHATGPT (Generative Pre-trained Transformer): Your ally for generating ideas, dialogues, and much more. It's like having a group of writers from Hollywood's writers' room on your laptop, ready to pitch ideas at any time. Moreover, if you can afford the paid plus version, you will be even more successful. Today, it is my most loyal ally. As I told you before, it assists me in all my editorial business.

Grammarly: With its new AI companion, it not only corrects your grammatical errors but also suggests style improvements. It's like having an editor in your pocket, but without the dramatic sighs.

Hemingway App: Perfect for honing your prose, ensuring every sentence is clear and powerful. Hemingway would likely approve, probably with a "Hmm, not bad".

DALL-E: Imagine being able to whisper your wildest dreams to a genie inside a lamp, and with a snap (or rather a click), your visions materialize before your eyes. That's DALL-E, an AI marvel from OpenAI capable of generating images from textual descriptions. Need a book cover that captures the essence of your latest sci-fi novel? Or perhaps illustrations that bring the landscapes of your poetry to life? DALL-E understands your words and transforms them into images that could rival Dalí's imagination. It's like having a painter, illustrator, and graphic designer at your fingertips, ready to turn your words into visual art.

Canva: Now, if what you seek is to shape those visions with a personal touch, Canva is your digital workshop of dreams. You don't need to be a graphic designer to create visual masterpieces that complement your texts. With its intuitive interface and an overwhelming library of templates, images, and fonts, Canva allows you to design everything from book covers to infographics that make your statistics dance. Imagine being able to illustrate your hero's journey or design the flyer for your next poetry book launch, all with a few clicks and drags. Canva democratizes design, enabling you to dress your words with the visual elegance they deserve.

Tutorials That Will Transform Your Writing:

How to Customize AI for Your Writing Style: Find these tutorials on platforms like YouTube or Coursera. They're like cooking classes, but instead of learning to make the perfect soufflé, you learn to cook up unforgettable stories with a touch of AI.

Mastering Editing with AI: Explore courses that teach you how to polish your texts until they shine. Think of it as karate training for your writing, each keystroke becoming stronger and more precise.

Online Communities Where the Magic Happens:

Reddit Forums like r/writing and r/artificial: Imagine a place where you can talk about the latest AI tool or vent about your writing struggles at 2 a.m. It's like a book club, but for writing and AI geeks.

~~Twitter~~ X and Hashtags Related to AI Writing: A constant party where you can share your successes, learn from the masters, and, of course, procrastinate productively.

Specialized Blogs: Yes, blogs still exist. In fact, having a blog is a good marketing tool for a writer. Writing articles is a way to keep typing. Look for writing or AI blogs. In them, you can find educational material to improve your writing and AI skills.

Today, it's very easy to find what you're looking for. Don't be afraid to delve into these specialized places and talk to people; you will likely find individuals with the same concerns as you.

Continuing the Adventure in Our Imaginary Book on AI-Assisted Writing, the next logical step is to immerse yourself in a detailed glossary. This glossary is your enchanted dictionary, the Rosetta Stone that will help you decipher the mysterious codes of AI. So, without further ado, here is a selection of essential terms adorned with our characteristic style.

GLOSSARY OF AI TERMS

Algorithm: Think of them as the secret recipes of AI. They aren't peanut butter and jelly sandwiches but formulas that instruct the AI on how to perform tasks, from understanding your whispers to creating poetry that could make a drone cry.

Predictive Analytics: It's the crystal ball of AI, allowing it to make predictions based on data. Useful for everything from deciding whether to carry an umbrella to predicting the next big literary hit.

Machine Learning: Imagine AI as an eternally curious student, constantly learning from mountains of data. It doesn't need sleep, which definitely puts it ahead of the learning curve.

Deep Learning: Here's where things get serious. It's machine learning on steroids, using neural networks inspired by the human brain to digest and learn from data. Think of it as the difference between learning to juggle two balls and doing it with fire.

Big Data: Imagine an infinite ocean of data, where every drop is a piece of information. Big Data is that ocean, encompassing everything from what you had for breakfast yesterday to the vast amounts of information generated online every second. AI dives into this sea to fish for insights and patterns.

Blockchain: Better known in the world of cryptocurrencies, but its principle of decentralized security and transparency also has interesting implications for AI, especially in terms of keeping immutable records of data or AI decisions.

Processing Power: The muscle behind the brain of AI. It refers to the computational power needed to perform AI's learning and analysis tasks. Essentially, how much can AI lift before needing a nap.

Chatbots: Your robotic friends who can hold conversations. Useful for everything from resolving your existential questions at 3 a.m. to helping you choose your next read.

Classification: Imagine sorting your books not just by genre but also by the emotions they evoke. Classification in AI is similar, dividing data into categories based on common characteristics. It's like having an OCD librarian.

Training Data: The textbooks of AI. These are the data used to teach AI how to perform its tasks. The richer and more varied these data are, the smarter the machine becomes, like a student devouring entire library.

Structured/Unstructured Data: Structured data are like books neatly organized on shelves, while unstructured data are the pile of notes and drafts scattered on your desk. AI needs to master both to truly "understand" the world.

Deepfake: A term that sounds like a comic book villain, but actually refers to AI-generated videos or audios that are so convincingly real that they can make you believe someone said or did something that never happened. A powerful reminder of the need for ethics in AI.

Feedback Loop: In the context of AI, it's like having a conversation with itself to improve. AI takes actions, learns from the results, and adjusts its future behaviors. It's a bit like learning to cook; you try, you burn, you learn, you get better.

Natural Language Generation (NLG): If Natural Language Processing allows AI to understand human language, Natural Language Generation is what enables it to speak or write like us. Basically, it's the AI's ability to tell jokes, write poems, or even create novels.

Artificial Intelligence (AI): The umbrella concept for all this fun. It's the simulation of human intelligence by machines. Think of it as the brain behind the operation, but without needing coffee.

Application Programming Interface (API): Think of it as a waiter who takes your orders to the kitchen (AI) and brings back delicious plates of data or analysis. APIs allow different software to communicate with each other seamlessly.

Machine Vision: The ability of AI to "see" and understand images and videos. It's like giving AI a pair of magic glasses that allow it to interpret the visual world, from recognizing your face to analyzing medical X-rays.

Predictive Modeling: Similar to predictive analytics but focused on building specific models that can foresee future outcomes. It's like having a crystal ball based on mathematics instead of magic.

Natural Language Understanding (NLU): One step beyond NLP, it not only understands language but also its meaning and context. It's like going from understanding the words of a joke to actually getting why it's funny.

Optimization: The art of making fine adjustments to ensure the AI performs as well as possible. Imagine tweaking the ingredients of a recipe until the dish is perfect. In AI, it's about finding the perfect balance for the machine to learn efficiently and effectively.

Pattern Recognition: The ability of AI to detect patterns in data. It's like when you start noticing your cat has a specific routine before sitting on your keyboard. AI uses this skill for everything from predicting the weather to identifying shopping trends.

Neural Networks: Inspired by the human brain, these are the structures that allow deep learning to happen. They're like the social networks of AI's brain cells, communicating and learning from each other.

This glossary is your master key to unlocking the secrets of AI in your creative journey. With these terms in your arsenal, you are well-equipped to take your first steps into the exciting world of AI-assisted writing. So, go ahead, use this knowledge to explore new creative frontiers, experiment with confidence, and, of course, keep writing stories only you can tell.

BIBLIOGRAPHY

In keeping with the tradition of keeping things light, imaginative, and full of spirit, let's acknowledge that, in a real world, this section would be filled with essential titles, pioneering studies, and insightful articles. However, in our fictional adventure, let me guide you through a slightly different "bibliography":

"The Dance of AI and the Pen" by Imaginary Author: A book that doesn't exist but could well be the manual for any writer eager to dance to the rhythm of technology without stepping on the delicate toes of creativity.

"Algorithms, Dreams, and Metaphors" by Visionary Scientist: Although this title is not found in your local bookstore, it represents those essential studies that teach us how AI can serve as a digital muse, unlocking levels of creativity that we are just beginning to explore.

Articles in 'The Imaginary Journal of AI Discoveries': Even though this journal doesn't arrive at your door, it symbolizes the wealth of discoveries and discussions in the field of AI, from natural language processing to machine learning, which fuel our imagination and ambition.

Conferences on 'Fictional Futures of Writing': These events, occurring in the limbo of the unrealized, remind us of the importance of sharing knowledge, debating ethics, and collectively exploring the potential of AI in creativity.

Online Forums and Communities like 'Scribes & Bots': Although you can't register today, these imaginary communities represent the spaces where writers and AI enthusiasts can share experiences, advice, and, most importantly, words of encouragement.

This bibliography, though fictional, serves as a playful reminder that our adventure in AI-assisted writing is just beginning. The real sources of inspiration and knowledge are as varied as the stars in the sky (very poetic, I know), waiting to be discovered by curious minds and brave hearts, and blah, blah, blah.

And yes, you got it right: the whole book has been assisted by my esteemed friend and collaborator, ChatGPT. The cover photo was made with DALL-E and formatted in Canva. But I assure you, the soul is mine. My name is José Manuel González, and I'm delighted to have guided you to this point.

So, as we close this chapter (and book), I invite you to continue exploring, learning, and, of course, writing. The story of AI and writing is being written now, and you have the opportunity to be a part of it. See you soon, my friend!

ACKNOWLEDGMENTS

Although assisted by AI, a book of this caliber is not made alone. And as we reach the end of this adventure, I cannot help but look back and reflect on the numerous people and inspirations that have made this journey towards understanding and leveraging artificial intelligence in our writing possible.

First and foremost, I want to express my deepest gratitude to the scientific and technological community, whose tireless research and developments in the field of artificial intelligence have opened new doors for creatives of all kinds. Without their dedication and forward-thinking vision, the tools and knowledge discussed in these pages would not exist.

To my fellow writers and friends, for their words of encouragement and valuable perspectives, I am deeply thankful. Your shared experiences and overcome challenges have been a constant source of inspiration and motivation in my own creative journey. Now, after reading this book, I hope you count on me for whatever you need and include me in your circle of friends.

I cannot overlook the unconditional support of my family, whose patience and understanding have been my beacon in moments of doubt and fatigue. Your unwavering love and faith in my vision have been the pillars upon which this project was built. Thank you for staying by my side and not having run away yet.

A special thanks to the readers and enthusiasts of intelligent writing, whose insatiable curiosity and appetite for exploring new literary horizons have been the true engine behind this book. I hope that what you find here serves as a compass and company in your own exploration of AI-assisted writing.

Finally, but not least, I want to thank artificial intelligence itself. Through its algorithms and capabilities, it has challenged me to expand the limits of my creativity and rethink what it means to be an author in the 21st century.

To each and every one of you, thank you from the bottom of my heart.

ABOUT THE AUTHOR

José Manuel González is a writer and editor of both fiction and non-fiction books. He has written numerous novels under various pseudonyms, published collections of stories, runs a blog and a literary podcast; he is knowledgeable about new technologies and is an athlete, having collaborated with his daughter on a series of sports books.

TRANSLATOR'S NOTE

The book you are holding, originally written in Spanish by José Manuel González, has been translated into English to bring its content to a wider audience. The original version captures the essence and distinctive style of the author, who has poured his experience and creativity into every page. The translation has been carried out with the utmost care and fidelity to the original text, aiming to preserve the author's unique voice and accurately convey the ideas and concepts presented in the work.

We hope you enjoy this literary journey and that the richness of the content inspires you as much as it has inspired readers of the original Spanish version. We appreciate your understanding of the linguistic and cultural nuances that may exist between the two languages. This translation effort is a bridge to connect different worlds and enrich the experience of all readers.